Congressional Research Service

Affirmative Action and Diversity in Public Education: Legal Developments

Jody Feder
Legislative Attorney

October 18, 2012

Congressional Research Service

7-5700

www.crs.gov

RL30410

CRS Report for Congress ————————————————————
Prepared for Members and Committees of Congress

Summary

More than three decades after the Supreme Court ruling in *Regents of the University of California v. Bakke*, the diversity rationale for affirmative action in public education remains a topic of political and legal controversy. Many colleges and universities have implemented affirmative action policies not only to remedy past discrimination, but also to achieve a racially and ethnically diverse student body or faculty. Justice Powell, in his opinion for the *Bakke* Court, stated that the attainment of a diverse student body is "a constitutionally permissible goal for an institution of higher education," noting that "[t]he atmosphere of 'speculation, experiment, and creation' so essential to the quality of higher education is widely believed to be promoted by a diverse student body." In subsequent years, however, federal courts began to question the Powell rationale, unsettling expectations about whether diversity-based affirmative action in educational admissions and faculty hiring is constitutional under the equal protection clause of the Fourteenth Amendment.

After a series of conflicting lower court rulings were issued regarding the use of race to promote a diverse student body, the Supreme Court agreed to review the race-conscious admissions policies used by the undergraduate and law school admissions programs at the University of Michigan. In *Grutter v. Bollinger*, a 5 to 4 majority of the Justices held that the University Law School had a "compelling" interest in the "educational benefits that flow from a diverse student body," which justified its race-based efforts to assemble a "critical mass" of "underrepresented" minority students. But in the companion decision, *Gratz v. Bollinger*, six Justices decided that the University's policy of awarding "racial bonus points" to minority applicants was not "narrowly tailored" enough to pass constitutional scrutiny. The decisions resolved, for the time being, the doctrinal muddle left in *Bakke*'s wake. And because the Court's constitutional holdings translate to the private sector under the federal civil rights laws, nonpublic schools, colleges, and universities are likewise affected.

However, the *Grutter* and *Gratz* decisions did not address whether diversity is a permissible goal in the elementary and secondary educational setting. To resolve this question, the Supreme Court agreed to review two cases that involved the use of race to maintain racially diverse public schools and to avoid racial segregation. In a consolidated 2007 ruling in *Parents Involved in Community Schools v. Seattle School District No. 1*, the Court struck down the Seattle and Louisville school plans at issue, holding that they violated the equal protection guarantee of the Fourteenth Amendment.

Meanwhile, the Court is poised to revisit the issue of affirmative action in higher education during the current 2012-2013 term. The case, *Fisher v. University of Texas*, involves an equal protection challenge to the undergraduate admissions plan at the University of Texas at Austin, which, in a stated effort to increase diversity, considers race as a factor when evaluating applicants to the school.

Contents

Contacts

I. Introduction

More than three decades after the Supreme Court ruling in *Regents of the University of California v. Bakke*,[1] the diversity rationale for affirmative action in public education remains a topic of political and legal controversy. Many colleges and universities have implemented affirmative action policies not only to remedy past discrimination, but also to achieve a racially and ethnically diverse student body or faculty. Justice Powell, in his opinion for the *Bakke* Court, stated that the attainment of a diverse student body is "a constitutionally permissible goal for an institution of higher education," noting that "[t]he atmosphere of 'speculation, experiment, and creation' so essential to the quality of higher education is widely believed to be promoted by a diverse student body."

In subsequent years, however, federal courts began to question the Powell rationale, unsettling expectations about whether diversity-based affirmative action in educational admissions and faculty hiring decisions is constitutional under the equal protection clause of the Fourteenth Amendment. In striking down the admissions process at the University of Texas School of Law, the U.S. Court of Appeals for the Fifth Circuit in *Hopwood v. Texas* concluded that any use of race in the admissions process was forbidden by the Constitution.[2] Reverberations of the 1996 *Hopwood* opinion are apparent in several subsequent cases, which voided "race conscious" policies maintained by institutions of higher education, as well as public elementary and secondary schools. Some judges avoided resolving the precedential effect of Justice Powell's opinion by deciding the case on "narrow tailoring" or other grounds not dependent on the constitutional status of student diversity as a compelling state interest.[3] But, in *Johnson v. Board of Regents*, the Eleventh Circuit sided with *Hopwood* by rejecting diversity as constitutional justification for a numerical "racial bonus" awarded minority freshman applicants to the University of Georgia. A circuit court conflict was created when the Ninth Circuit relied on *Bakke* to uphold an affirmative action admissions policy to the University of Washington Law School that made extensive use of race-based factors. *Smith v. University of Washington* was the first federal appeals court to rely on Justice Powell's decision as binding precedent on the issue.[4]

---

[1] 438 U.S. 265 (1978).

[2] 78 F.3d 932, 944 (5th Cir. 1996) ("Justice Powell's view in *Bakke* is not binding precedent on the issue."), cert. denied, 518 U.S. 1033 (1996). See also Lutheran Church-Missouri Synod v. FCC, 141 F.3d 344, 354 (D.C.Cir. 1998) (stating, without addressing *Bakke*, that diversity cannot "be elevated to the 'compelling' level").

[3] See Brewer v. West Irondequoit Center School District, 212 F.3d 738, 747-49 (2d Cir. 2000) (noting that "there is much disagreement among the circuit courts as to ... the state of the law under current Supreme Court jurisprudence," but concluding that, regardless of *Bakke*, reducing racial isolation may be a compelling interest under Second Circuit precedent); Eisenberg v. Montgomery County Public Schools, 197 F.3d 123, 130 (4th Cir. 1999) (explaining that the status of educational diversity as a compelling interest is "unresolved," and rather than rule on the issue, decided the case solely on narrow tailoring grounds); Wessmann v. Gittens, 160 F.3d 790, 795, 800 (1st Cir. 1998) (While "[t]he question of precisely what interests government may legitimately invoke to justify race-based classifications is largely unsettled," the court concluded defendant's apparent interest in "racial balancing" of the student body was neither "a legitimate [n]or necessary means of advancing" diversity); Buchwald v. University of New Mexico School of Medicine, 159 F.3d 487, 499 (10th Cir. 1998) (noting the absence of "a clear majority opinion" in *Bakke*, but according qualified immunity to defendants who relied upon that case in adopting a preference based on durational residency); McNamara v. City of Chicago, 138 F.3d 1219, 1222 (7th Cir. 1998) (citing *Bakke* for statement that "whether there may be compelling interests other than remedying past discrimination remains 'unsettled,'" but finding defendant's remedial justification valid).

[4] Smith v. University of Washington Law School, 233 F.3d 1188, 1201 (9th Cir. 2000) (pursuant to *Bakke*, "educational diversity is a compelling governmental interest that meets the demands of strict scrutiny of race conscious measures"), cert. denied, 532 U.S. 1051 (2001).

The judicial divide over *Bakke*'s legacy was vividly underscored by a pair of separate trial court decisions, one upholding for diversity reasons the race-based undergraduate admissions policy of the University of Michigan,[5] the other voiding a special minority law school admissions program at the same institution.[6] Restoring a degree of clarity to the law, the U.S. Supreme Court concluded its 2002-2003 term with rulings in the Michigan cases. In *Grutter v. Bollinger*,[7] a 5 to 4 majority of the Justices held that the law school had a "compelling" interest in the "educational benefits that flow from a diverse student body," which justified its consideration of race in admissions to assemble a "critical mass" of "underrepresented" minority students. But in a companion decision, *Gratz v. Bollinger*,[8] six Justices decided that the university's policy of awarding "racial bonus points" to minority applicants was not "narrowly tailored" enough to pass constitutional scrutiny.

However, the *Grutter* and *Gratz* decisions did not address whether diversity is a permissible goal in the elementary and secondary educational setting. To resolve this question, the Supreme Court agreed to review two cases that involved the use of race to maintain racially diverse public schools. The cases were *Meredith v. Jefferson County Board of Education*—formerly *MacFarland v. Jefferson County Public Schools*—and *Parents Involved in Community Schools v. Seattle School District No. 1*.[9] In *Parents Involved in Community Schools v. Seattle School District No. 1*, a consolidated 2007 ruling that resolved both cases, the Court ultimately struck down the school plans at issue, holding that they violated the equal protection guarantee of the Fourteenth Amendment.[10]

Meanwhile, the Court is poised to revisit the issue of affirmative action in higher education during the current 2012-2013 term. The case, *Fisher v. University of Texas*,[11] involves an equal protection challenge to the undergraduate admissions plan at the University of Texas at Austin, which, in a stated effort to increase diversity, considers race as a factor when evaluating applicants to the school.

The first part of this report briefly reviews the judicial evolution of race-based affirmative action, particularly in relation to public education. The report then reviews major rulings involving challenges to the use of race-conscious admissions and hiring practices by public educational institutions, and concludes with a discussion of the implications for the future development of affirmative action law.

II. Historical Background

The origins of affirmative action law may be traced to the early 1960s as first the Warren, and then the Burger Court, grappled with the seemingly intractable problem of racial segregation in

---

[5] Gratz v. Bollinger, 122 F.Supp.2d 811 (E.D.Mich. 2000).

[6] Grutter v. Bollinger, 137 F. Supp. 2d 821, 848 (E.D. Mich. 2001) (concluding that "*Bakke* does not stand for the proposition that a university's desire to assemble a racially diverse student body is a compelling state interest").

[7] 539 U.S. 306 (2003).

[8] 539 U.S. 244 (2003).

[9] 416 F.3d 513 (6th Cir. 2003) (per curiam), cert. granted, 547 U.S. 1177 (2006); 426 F.3d 1162 (9th Cir. 2005) (en banc), cert. granted, 547 U.S. 1177 (2006).

[10] 551 U.S. 701 (2007).

[11] 132 S. Ct. 1536 (2012).

the nation's public schools. Judicial rulings from this period recognized an "affirmative duty," cast upon local school boards by the Equal Protection Clause, to desegregate formerly "dual school" systems and to eliminate "root and branch" the last "vestiges" of state-enforced segregation.[12] These holdings ushered in a two-decade era of "massive" desegregation—first in the South, and later the urban North—marked by federal desegregation orders frequently requiring drastic reconfiguration of school attendance patterns along racial lines and extensive student transportation schemes. School districts across the nation operating under these decrees have since sought to be declared in compliance with constitutional requirements in order to gain release from federal intervention. The Supreme Court eventually responded by holding that judicial control of a school system previously found guilty of intentional segregation should be relinquished if, looking to all aspects of school operations, it appears that the district has complied with desegregation requirements in "good faith" for a "reasonable period of time" and has eliminated "vestiges" of past discrimination "to the extent practicable."[13]

A statutory framework for affirmative action in employment and education was enacted by the Civil Rights Act of 1964. Public and private employers with 15 or more employees are subject to a comprehensive code of equal employment opportunity regulations under Title VII of the 1964 act. The Title VII remedial scheme rests largely on judicial power to order monetary damages and injunctive relief, including "such affirmative action as may be appropriate,"[14] to make discrimination victims whole. Except as may be imposed by court order or consent decree to remedy past discrimination, however, there is no general statutory obligation on employers to adopt affirmative action remedies. But the Equal Employment Opportunity Commission (EEOC) has issued guidelines to protect employers and unions from charges of "reverse discrimination" when they voluntarily take action to correct the effects of past discrimination.[15]

The term "affirmative action" resurfaced in federal regulations construing the 1964 act's Title VI, which prohibits racial or ethnic discrimination in all federally assisted "programs" and activities,[16] including public or private educational institutions. The Office of Civil Rights of the Department of Education interpreted Title VI to require schools and colleges to take affirmative action to overcome the effects of past discrimination and to encourage "voluntary affirmative action to attain a diverse student body."[17] Another Title VI regulation permits a college or university to take racial or national origin into account when awarding financial aid if the aid is necessary to overcome effects of past institutional discrimination.[18] Affirmative action in higher

---

[12] See e.g. Green v. County Board, 391 U.S. 430 (1968); Swann v. Board of Education, 402 U.S. 1 (1971); Keyes v. Denver School District, 413 U.S. 189 (1973).

[13] Dowell v. Board of Education, 498 U.S. 237 (1991). See also Freeman v. Pitts, 503 U.S. 467 (1993) (allowing incremental dissolution of judicial control) and Missouri v. Jenkins, 515 U.S. 70 (1995) (directing district court on remand to "bear in mind that its end purpose is not only 'to remedy the violation' to the extent practicable, but also 'to restore state and local authorities to the control of a school system that is operating in compliance with the Constitution.'").

[14] 42 U.S.C. 2000e-5(g).

[15] 29 C.F.R. Part 1608 (the guidelines state the EEOC's position that when employers voluntarily undertake in good faith to remedy past discrimination by race- or gender-conscious affirmative action means, the agency will not find them liable for reverse discrimination.).

[16] 42 U.S.C. 2000d et seq.

[17] 44 Fed. Reg. 58,509 (October 10, 1979).

[18] 59 Fed. Reg. 8756 (February 23, 1994). See also Letter from Judith A. Winston, General Counsel, United States Department of Education, to College and University Counsel, July 30, 1996 (reaffirming that it is permissible in appropriate circumstances for colleges and universities to consider race in admissions decisions and granting financial aid).

education was before Congress in 1998, when the full House defeated a bill to prohibit federal aid to colleges and universities that consider race, ethnicity, or sex in the admission process.

The *Bakke* ruling in 1978 launched the contemporary constitutional debate over state-sponsored affirmative action. A "notable lack of unanimity" was evident from the six separate opinions filed in that case. One four-Justice plurality in *Bakke* voted to strike down as a violation of Title VI a special admissions program of the University of California at Davis medical school which set aside 16 of 100 positions in each incoming class for minority students, where the institution itself was not shown to have discriminated in the past. Another bloc of four Justices argued that racial classifications designed to further remedial purposes were foreclosed neither by the Constitution nor the Civil Rights Act and would have upheld the minority admissions quota. Justice Powell added a fifth vote to each camp by condemning the Davis program on equal protection grounds while endorsing the nonexclusive consideration of race as an admissions criterion to foster student diversity.

In Justice Powell's view, neither the state's asserted interest in remedying "societal discrimination," nor of providing "role models" for minority students was sufficiently "compelling" to warrant the use of a "suspect" racial classification in the admission process. But the attainment of a "diverse student body" was, for Justice Powell, "clearly a permissible goal for an institution of higher education" since diversity of minority viewpoints furthered "academic freedom," a "special concern of the First Amendment."[19] Accordingly, race could be considered by a university as a "plus" or "one element of a range of factors"—even if it "tipped the scale" among qualified applicants—as long as it "did not insulate the individual from comparison with all the other candidates for the available seats."[20] The "quota" in *Bakke* was infirm, however, since it defined diversity only in racial terms and absolutely excluded non-minorities from a given number of seats. By two 5-to-4 votes, therefore, the Supreme Court affirmed the lower court order admitting Bakke but reversed the judicial ban on consideration of race in admissions.

Bakke was followed by *Wygant v. Jackson Board of Education*,[21] where a divided Court ruled unconstitutional the provision of a collective bargaining agreement that protected minority public school teachers from layoff at the expense of more senior white faculty members. While holding the specific layoff preference for minority teachers unconstitutional, seven *Wygant* Justices seemed to agree in principle that a governmental employer is not prohibited by the Equal Protection Clause from all race-conscious affirmative action to remedy its own past discrimination. Another series of decisions approved of congressionally mandated racial preferences to allocate the benefits of contracts on federally sponsored public works projects,[22] and in the design of certain broadcast licensing schemes,[23] while condemning similar actions taken by local governmental entities to promote public contracting opportunities for minority entrepreneurs.[24] However, in each of these cases, the Justices failed to achieve a consensus on most issues, with bare majorities, pluralities, or—as in *Bakke*—a single Justice, determining the outcome of the case.

---

[19] Regents of Univ. of Cal. v. Bakke, 438 U.S. 265, 311-12 (1978).

[20] *Id.* at 317.

[21] 476 U.S. 267 (1986).

[22] Fullilove v. Klutznick, 448 U.S. 448 (1980).

[23] Metro Broadcasting, Inc. v. FCC, 497 U.S. 547 (1990).

[24] City of Richmond v. J.A. Croson Co., 488 U.S. 469 (1989).

By the mid-1980s, the Supreme Court had approved the temporary remedial use of race- or gender-conscious selection criteria by private employers under Title VII of the 1964 Civil Rights Act.[25] These measures were deemed a proper remedy for "manifest racial imbalance" in "traditionally segregated" job categories, if voluntarily adopted by the employer,[26] or for entrenched patterns of "egregious and longstanding" discrimination by the employer, if imposed by judicial decree.[27] In either circumstance, however, the Court required proof of remedial justification rooted in the employer's own past discrimination and its persistent workplace effects. Thus, a "firm basis" in evidence, as revealed by a "manifest imbalance"—or "historic," "persistent," and "egregious" underrepresentation—of minorities or women in affected job categories was deemed an essential predicate to preferential affirmative action. Second, but of equal importance, all racial preferences in employment were to be judged in terms of their adverse impact on "identifiable" non-minority group members. Remedies that protected minorities from layoff, for example, were most suspect and unlikely to pass legal or constitutional muster if they displaced more senior white workers. But the consideration of race or gender as a "plus" factor in employment decisions, when it did not unduly hinder or "trammel" the "legitimate expectations" of non-minority employees, won ready judicial acceptance.[28] Affirmative action preferences, however, had to be sufficiently flexible, temporary in duration, and "narrowly tailored" to avoid becoming rigid "quotas."

Not until 1989, however, did a majority of the Justices resolve the proper constitutional standard for reviewing equal protection challenges to governmental classifications by race enacted for a remedial or other "benign" legislative purpose. Disputes prior to *City of Richmond v. J.A. Croson*[29] yielded divergent views as to whether state affirmative action measures for the benefit of racial minorities were subject to the same "strict scrutiny" as applied to "invidious" racial discrimination under the Equal Protection Clause, an "intermediate" standard resembling the test for gender-based classifications, or simple rationality. In *Croson*, a 5 to 4 majority settled on strict scrutiny to invalidate a 30% set-aside of city contracts for minority-owned businesses because the program was not "narrowly tailored" to a "compelling" governmental interest. While "race-conscious" remedies could be legislated in response to proven past discrimination by the affected governmental entities, "racial balancing" untailored to "specific" and "identified" evidence of minority exclusion was impermissible. *Croson* suggested, however, that because of its unique equal protection enforcement authority, a constitutional standard more tolerant of racial line-drawing may apply to Congress. This conclusion was reinforced a year later when, in *Metro Broadcasting, Inc. v. FCC*,[30] the Court upheld certain minority broadcast licensing schemes approved by Congress to promote the "important" governmental interest in "broadcast diversity."

The two-tiered approach to equal protection analysis of governmental affirmative action was short-lived. In *Adarand Constructors, Inc. v. Pena*,[31] the Court applied "strict scrutiny" to a federal transportation program of financial incentives for prime contractors who subcontracted to firms owned by "socially and economically disadvantaged individuals," defined so as to prefer members of designated racial minorities. Although the Court refrained from deciding the

---

[25] 42 U.S.C. §§ 2000e et seq.

[26] United Steelworkers v. Weber, 443 U.S. 193 (1979).

[27] Local 28 Sheet Metal Workers v. EEOC, 478 U.S. 421 (1986).

[28] United States v. Paradise, 480 U.S. 149 (1987); Johnson v. Transportation Agency, 480 U.S. 616 (1987).

[29] 488 U.S. 469 (1989).

[30] 497 U.S. 547 (1990).

[31] 515 U.S. 200 (1995).

constitutional merits of the particular program before it, and remanded for further proceedings below, it determined that all "racial classifications" by government at any level must be justified by a "compelling governmental interest" and "narrowly tailored" to that end. But the majority opinion sought to "dispel the notion" that "strict scrutiny is 'strict in theory, but fatal in fact,'" by acknowledging a role for Congress as architect of remedies for discrimination nationwide. "The unhappy persistence of both the practices and lingering effects of racial discrimination against minorities in this country is an unfortunate reality, and the government is not disqualified from acting in response to it." No further guidance is provided, however, as to the scope of remedial power remaining in congressional hands, or of the conditions required for its exercise. Bottom line, *Adarand* suggests that racial preferences in federal law or policy are a remedy of last resort and must be adequately justified and narrowly drawn to pass constitutional muster.

III. Legal Developments

Over the years, the Supreme Court has addressed the constitutionality of affirmative action in a number of educational contexts, including higher education, elementary and secondary education, and faculty hiring. Each of these contexts is discussed separately below.

Student Diversity in Higher Education Admissions

Beginning with *Bakke*, the Court has heard three different challenges to race-conscious admissions plans at institutions of higher education, and is currently poised to review the issue yet again in the upcoming *Fisher v. University of Texas* case.

Regents of the University of California v. Bakke

The emphasis in *Adarand* on past discrimination prompted a surge in judicial challenges to educational diversity as an independent justification for student and faculty affirmative action. The notion that diversity could rise to the level of a compelling interest in the educational setting sprang a quarter century ago from Justice Powell's opinion in the *Bakke* case. While concluding that a state medical school could not set-aside a certain number of seats for minority applicants, Justice Powell opined that a diverse student body may serve educators' legitimate interest in promoting the "robust" exchange of ideas. He cautioned, however, that "[t]he diversity that furthers a compelling state interest encompasses a far broader array of qualifications and characteristics of which ethnic origin is but a single though important element."[32]

Justice Powell split the difference between two four-Justice pluralities in *Bakke*. One camp, led by Justice Stevens, struck down the admissions quota on statutory civil rights grounds. Another led by Justice Brennan would have upheld the medical school's policy as a remedy for societal discrimination. Justice Powell held the "dual admissions" procedure to be unconstitutional, and ordered Bakke's admission. But, he concluded, that the state's interest in educational diversity could warrant consideration of students' race in certain circumstances. For Justice Powell, a diverse student body fostered the "robust" exchange of ideas and academic freedom deserving of constitutional protection.

---

[32] Regents of Univ. of Cal. v. Bakke, 438 U.S. 265, 315 (1978).

Justice Powell's theory of diversity as a compelling governmental interest did not turn on race alone. He pointed with approval to the "Harvard Plan," which defined diversity in terms of a broad array of factors and characteristics. Thus, an applicant's race could be deemed a "plus" factor. It was considered on a par with personal talents, leadership qualities, family background, or any other factor contributing to a diverse student body. However, the race of a candidate could not be the "sole" or "determinative" factor. No other Justice joined in the Powell opinion.

Although Justice Powell's opinion announced the judgment of the Court, no other *Bakke* Justices joined him on that point. Justice Powell ruled the "dual admission program" at issue to be unconstitutional and the white male plaintiff entitled to admission, while four other Justices reached the same result on statutory rather than constitutional grounds. Another four Justice plurality concluded that the challenged policy was lawful, but agreed with Justice Powell that the state court had erred by holding that an applicant's race could never be taken into account. Only Justice Powell, therefore, expressed the view that the attainment of a diverse student body could be a compelling state interest.

For nearly two decades, colleges and universities relied on the Powell opinion in *Bakke* to support race-conscious student diversity policies. Consideration of race in admissions, which took various forms, stood pretty much unchallenged until *Hopwood v. State of Texas.*[33] A panel of the Fifth Circuit repudiated the Powell diversity rationale when it voided a special admission program of the University of Texas law school. Unlike *Bakke*, the Texas program entailed no explicit racial quota. But, in other respects, it was a classic dual track system: one standard for blacks and Hispanics, another for everyone else, and cutoff scores for minorities were lower. The Powell opinion was not binding precedent, the *Hopwood* panel ruled, since it was not joined by any other Justice. Thus, race could be considered in admissions only to remedy past discrimination by the law school itself, which was not shown in *Hopwood*.

Several other federal circuit courts, besides the Sixth Circuit in the Michigan case, looked at race-based college admissions after *Bakke*. *Johnson v. Board of Regents*[34] struck down the award of "racial bonus" points to minority students as one of 12 factors—academic and nonacademic— considered for freshman admissions to the University of Georgia. The Eleventh Circuit majority was skeptical of the Powell opinion but did not take a stand on the diversity issue. Instead, the program failed the second requirement of strict scrutiny. It was not "narrowly tailored." That is, it "mechanically awards an arbitrary 'diversity' bonus to each and every non-white applicant at a decisive stage in the admissions process." At the same time, the policy arbitrarily limited the number of nonracial factors that could be considered, all at the expense of white applicants, even those whose social or economic background and personal traits would promote "experiential" diversity. On the other hand, the Ninth Circuit upheld the minority law school admissions program at the University of Washington on the basis of *Bakke*. The appeals court in *Smith v. University of Washington Law School*[35] concluded that the four Brennan Justices who approved of the racial quota in *Bakke* "would have embraced [the diversity rationale] if need be." Justice Powell's opinion thus became the "narrowest footing" for approval of race in admission and was the "holding" of *Bakke*.

---

[33] 78 F.3d 932 (5ᵗʰ Cir. 1996), cert. denied 518 U.S. 1033 (1996).

[34] 263 F.3d 1234 (11ᵗʰ Cir. 2001).

[35] 233 F.3d 1188 (9ᵗʰ Cir. 2000).

Post-*Bakke* appeals courts, guided by *Marks v. United States*,[36] sliced and diced the various opinions in *Bakke* to come up with a controlling rationale. In *Marks*, the Supreme Court ruled that when a majority of Justices are unable to agree on a controlling rationale, the holding of the Court is the position of those Justices concurring in the judgment on the narrowest grounds. The pro-diversity circuits concluded that the Powell opinion approving race as a "plus" factor was narrower than the Brennan rationale, which would have upheld the race quota in *Bakke* on a societal discrimination theory. The opposing circuits had generally reasoned otherwise or concluded that the competing *Bakke* opinions defy rational comparison so that absent a majority consensus, the Powell opinion was without controlling weight. In no way bound by *Bakke*, Supreme Court review of the Michigan cases augured fundamental reexamination of issues raised by that earlier precedent.

Background in the University of Michigan Admissions Cases

The judicial divide over the student diversity policies deepened with the University of Michigan cases. One federal district court in *Grutter* originally struck down the student diversity policy of the University of Michigan Law School, while another judge upheld a procedure awarding points to "underrepresented minority" applicants to the undergraduate school.[37] Based on *Bakke*, the Sixth Circuit reversed *Grutter* and permitted the law school to consider race in admissions.[38] The Supreme Court granted *certiorari* in *Grutter* and agreed to review *Gratz* prior to judgment by the Sixth Circuit.

Undergraduate admission to the University of Michigan had been based on a point system or "student selection index." A total possible 150 points could be awarded for factors, academic and otherwise, that made up the selection index. Academic factors accounted for up to 110 points, including 12 for standardized test performance. By comparison, 20 points could be awarded for one, but only one, of the following: membership in an underrepresented minority group, socioeconomic disadvantage, or athletics. Applicants could receive one to four points for "legacy" or alumni relationships, three points for personal essay, five points for community leadership and service, six points for in-state residency, etc. In practice, students at the extremes of academic performance were typically admitted or rejected on that basis alone. But for the middle range of qualified applicants, these other factors were often determinative. Finally, counselors could "flag" applications for review by the Admissions Review Committee, where any factor important to the freshman class composition—race included—was not adequately reflected in the selection index score.

In upholding this policy, the district court in *Gratz* found that *Bakke* and the University's own evidence demonstrating the educational benefits of racial and ethnic diversity established a compelling state interest. And the award of 20 points for minority status was not a "quota" or "dual track" system, as in *Bakke*, but only a "plus factor," to be weighed against others in the selection process. Thus, the constitutional demand for "narrow tailoring" was satisfied. The *Gratz* district court also concluded that "vigorous minority recruitment" and other race-neutral alternatives to the current policy would not yield a "sufficiently diverse student body."

---

[36] 430 U.S. 188 (1977).

[37] Gratz v. Bollinger, 122 F. Supp. 811 (E.D. Mich. 2000).

[38] Grutter v. Bollinger, 288 F.3d 732 (6th Cir. 2002).

Generally setting the bar for admission to the Michigan Law School was a "selection index" based on applicants' composite LSAT score and undergraduate GPA. A 1992 policy statement, however, made an explicit commitment to "racial and ethnic diversity," seeking to enroll a "critical mass" of black, Mexican-American, and Native American students. The objective was to enroll minority students in sufficient numbers to enable their participation in classroom discussions without feeling "isolated or like spokesmen for their race." To foster, "distinctive perspectives and experiences," admission officers consider a range of "soft variables"—for example, talents, interests, experiences, and "underrepresented minority" status—in their admissions decisions. In the course of each year's admissions process, the record showed, minority admission rates were regularly reported to track "the racial composition of the developing class." The 1992 policy replaced an earlier "special admissions program," which set a written goal of 10%-12% minority enrollment and lower academic requirements for those groups. The district court in *Grutter* made several key findings: there is a "heavy emphasis" on race in the law school admissions process; that over a period of time (1992-1998) minorities ranged from 11% to 17% of each incoming class; and that large numbers of minority students were admitted with index scores the same as or lower than unsuccessful white applicants.

Writing for the Sixth Circuit majority, Judge Martin adopted the Powell position in *Bakke* to find that the law school had a compelling interest in achieving a racially diverse student body, and that its admission's policy was "narrowly tailored" to that end. "Soft variables" were found to treat each applicant as an individual and to be "virtually indistinguishable" from "plus factors" and the Harvard Plan approved by Justice Powell in *Bakke*. The law school's policy "did not set-aside or reserve" seats on the basis of race. Rather, in pursuit of a "critical mass," the policy was designed to ensure that a "meaningful number" of minority students were able "to contribute to classroom dialogue without feeling isolated." The majority opinion further emphasized that the admissions program was "flexible," with no "fixed goal or target"; that it did not use "separate tracks" for minority and nonminority candidates; and did not function as a "quota system."

Without waiting for a final appeals court decision, the Supreme Court agreed to review the *Gratz* undergraduate admissions case in tandem with the Sixth Circuit ruling in *Grutter*. The Supreme Court handed down its rulings in *Grutter* and *Gratz* in 2003. Writing for the majority in the former was Justice O'Connor, who was joined by Justices Stevens, Souter, Ginsburg, and Breyer in upholding the law school admissions policy. Chief Justice Rehnquist authored an opinion, in which Justices O'Connor, Scalia, Kennedy, and Thomas joined, striking down the university's undergraduate racial admissions program. Justice Breyer added a sixth vote to invalidate the racial bonus system in *Gratz*, but declined to join the majority opinion.

The Grutter Decision

A notable aspect of the *Grutter* majority opinion was the degree to which it echoed the Powell rationale from *Bakke*. Settling, for the present, the doctrinal imbroglio that had consumed so much recent lower court attention, Justice O'Connor quoted extensively from Justice Powell's opinion, finding it to be the "touchstone for constitutional analysis of race-conscious admissions policies." But her opinion was not without its own possible doctrinal innovations. Overarching much of her reasoning were two paramount themes, that drew considerable criticism from Justice Thomas and his fellow dissenters. First, in applying "strict scrutiny" to the racial aspects of the law school admissions program, Justice O'Connor stressed the situational nature of constitutional interpretation, taking "relevant differences into account." Thus, the majority opined, "[c]ontext matters when reviewing race-based governmental action" for equal protection purposes and "[n]ot every decision influenced by race is equally objectionable," but may depend upon "the importance and the sincerity of the reasons advanced by the governmental decisionmaker" for that particular use of race. Second, and equally significant, was the deference accorded to the judgment of educational decision-makers in defining the scope of their academic mission, even in regard to matters of racial and ethnic diversity. "[U]niversities occupy a special niche in our constitutional tradition," Justice O'Connor stated, such that "[t]he Law School's educational judgment ... that diversity is essential to its educational mission is one to which we defer." Institutional "good faith" would be "presumed" in the absence of contrary evidence. Justice Thomas's dissent, joined by Justice Scalia, took particular exception to what he viewed as "the fundamentally flawed proposition that racial discrimination can be contextualized"—deemed "compelling" for one purpose but not another—or that strict scrutiny permits "any sort of deference" to "the Law School's conclusion that its racial experimentation leads to educational benefits." Indeed, the dissenters found such deference to be "antithetical" to the level of searching review demanded by strict scrutiny.

Satisfied that the law school had "compelling" reasons for pursuing a racially diverse student body, the Court moved to the second phase of strict scrutiny analysis. "Narrow tailoring," as noted, requires a close fit between "means" and "end" when the state draws any distinction based on race. In *Grutter*, the concept of "critical mass," so troubling to several Justices at oral argument, won the majority's approval as "necessary to further its compelling interest in securing the educational benefits of a diverse student body." In this portion of her opinion, Justice O'Connor drew chapter and verse from the standards articulated by Justice Powell in *Bakke*.

> We find that the Law School's admissions program bears the hallmarks of a narrowly tailored plan. As Justice Powell made clear in *Bakke*, truly individualized consideration demands that race be used in a flexible, nonmechanical way. It follows from this mandate that universities cannot establish quotas for members of certain racial groups or put members of those groups on separate admissions tracks. Nor can universities insulate applicants who belong to certain racial or ethnic groups from the competition for admission. Universities can, however, consider race or ethnicity more flexibly as a "plus" factor in the context of individualized consideration of each and every applicant.

Justice O'Connor drew a key distinction between forbidden "quotas" and permitted "goals," exonerating the law school's admission program from constitutional jeopardy. She observed that both approaches pay "some attention to numbers." But while the former are "fixed" and "reserved exclusively for certain minority groups," the opinion continued, the law school's "goal of attaining a critical mass" of minority students required only a "good faith effort" by the institution. In addition, Justice O'Connor noted, minority law school enrollment between 1993 and 2000 varied from 13.5% to 20.1%, "a range inconsistent with a quota." Responding, in his separate dissent, the Chief Justice objected that the notion of a "critical mass" was a "sham," or subterfuge for "racial balancing," since it did not explain disparities in the proportion of the three minority groups admitted under its auspices.

Other factors further persuaded the Court that the law school admissions process was narrowly tailored. By avoiding racial or ethnic "bonuses," the policy permitted consideration of "all pertinent elements of diversity," racial and nonracial, in "a highly individualized, holistic review of each applicant's file." Justice O'Connor also found that "race neutral alternatives" had been "sufficiently considered" by the law school, although few specific examples are provided. Importantly, however, the opinion made plain that "exhaustion" of "every conceivable alternative" is not constitutionally required, only a "serious good faith consideration of workable race-neutral alternatives that will achieve the diversity the university seeks." Consequently, the law school was not required to consider a lottery or lowering of traditional academic benchmarks—GPA and LSAT scores—for all applicants since "these alternatives would require a dramatic sacrifice of diversity, the academic quality of all admitted students, or both." And, because the admissions program was based on individual assessment of all pertinent elements of diversity, it did not "unduly burden" non-minority applicants. Nonetheless, as she had during oral argument, Justice O'Connor emphasized the need for "reasonable durational provisions," and "periodic reviews" by institutions conducting such programs. To drive home the point, the majority concludes with a general admonition. "We expect that 25 years from now, the use of racial preferences will no longer be necessary to further the interest approved today."

Besides Justices Thomas and Scalia, and the Chief Justice, another dissenting opinion was filed by Justice Kennedy, who agreed with his brethren that the "constancy" of minority admissions over a period of years "raised a suspicion" of racial balancing that the law school was required by the rigors of strict scrutiny to rebut. Arguing from different statistics than the majority, he found "little deviation among admitted minority students from 1995 to 1998," which "fluctuated only by 0.3% from 13.5% to 13.8" and "at no point fell below 12%, historically defined by the Law School as the bottom of its critical mass range." In addition, he contended, the use of daily reports on minority admissions near the end of the process shifted the focus from individualized review of each applicant to institutional concerns for the numerical objective defined by a "critical mass." For these reasons, he agreed with his fellow dissenters that deference to the law school in this situation was "antithetical to strict scrutiny, not consistent with it."

The Gratz Decision

The four *Grutter* dissenters were joined by Justices O'Conner and Breyer in striking down the racial bonus system for undergraduate admissions in *Gratz*. Basically, the same factors that saved the law school policy, by their absence, conspired to condemn the undergraduate program, in the eyes of the majority. Since the university's "compelling" interest in racial student diversity was settled in *Grutter*, the companion case focused on the reasons why the automatic award of 20 admission points to minority applicants failed the narrow tailoring aspect of strict scrutiny analysis. Relying, again, on the Powell rationale in *Bakke*, the policy was deemed more than a "plus" factor, as it denied each applicant "individualized consideration" by making race "decisive" for "virtually every minimally qualified underrepresented minority applicant." Nor did the procedure for "flagging" individual applications for additional review rescue the policy since "such consideration is the exception and not the rule," occurring—if at all—only after the "bulk of admission decisions" are made based on the point system. The opinion of the Chief Justice rejected the university's argument based on "administrative convenience," that the volume of freshman applications makes it "impractical" to apply a more individualized review. "[T]he fact that the implementation of a program capable of providing individualized consideration might present administrative challenges does not render constitutional an otherwise problematic system." Finally, the majority made plain that its constitutional holding in *Gratz* is fully applicable to private colleges and universities pursuant to the federal civil rights laws. "We have explained that discrimination that violates the Equal Protection Clause of the Fourteenth Amendment committed by an institution that accepts federal funds also constitutes a violation of Title VI [of the 1964 Civil Rights Act]."

Justice O'Connor, concurring in *Gratz*, emphasized the "mechanical" and "automatic" nature of the selection index scoring, which distinguished it from the law school program, and made impossible any "nuanced judgments" concerning "the particular background, experiences, or qualities of each particular candidate." She agreed that the Admissions Review Committee was "kind of an afterthought," particularly since the record was barren of evidence concerning its methods of operation and "how the decisions are actually made."

Dissenting opinions were filed jointly, by Justices Stevens and Souter, and separately by Justice Ginsburg. The former argued on technical grounds that since the named petitioners had already enrolled in other schools, and were not presently seeking freshman admission at the university, they lacked standing to seek prospective relief and the appeal should be dismissed. But Justice Souter argued separately on the merits that the Michigan undergraduate admission program was sufficiently different from the racial quota in *Bakke* to be constitutionally acceptable. At the very least, he felt, a more appropriate course would be to remand the case for further development of the record to determine whether the entire "admissions process, including review by the [Admissions Review Committee], results in individualized review sufficient to meet the Court's standards." Justice Ginsburg found "no constitutional infirmity" in the Michigan program since only "qualified" applicants are admitted, the current policy is not intended "to limit or decrease" admissions of any racial or ethnic group, and admissions of nonminority groups are not "unduly restricted." More broadly, she opined that government decision-makers may properly distinguish between policies of inclusion and exclusion, because the former are more likely to comport with constitutional imperatives of individual equality.

The Upcoming *Fisher v. University of Texas* Case

This coming term, the Court will revisit the issue of affirmative action in higher education for the first time since *Grutter* and *Gratz* were decided in 2003. The case, *Fisher v. University of Texas*,[39] involves an equal protection challenge to the undergraduate admissions plan at the University of Texas at Austin (UT), which, in a stated effort to increase diversity, considers race as a factor when evaluating applicants to the school.

The use of racial preferences in UT admissions has a complicated history. For many years, UT admitted students based on a simple formula that considered students solely on the basis of academic achievement and race. In 1996, however, the university was forced to abandon this admissions program in the wake of *Hopwood v. Texas*,[40] an appellate decision holding that Justice Powell's opinion in *Bakke* was not controlling and that UT's race-conscious plan was unconstitutional. After this decision, Texas adopted a new Top Ten Percent (TTP) plan, which requires state universities to automatically admit any student who graduated from a state high school in the top 10% of his or her class. In general, approximately 80% of each class was admitted under this approach, while the remaining students were selected based on a number of race-neutral criteria measuring academic and personal achievement, including essays, leadership, awards and honors, work experience, extracurricular activities, community service, and special circumstances such as socioeconomic status or family responsibilities.

This race-neutral approach significantly increased minority enrollment at Texas universities, although disparities remained within certain majors and classrooms. However, in the wake of *Grutter*, UT reintroduced race as a factor as part of the evaluation of personal achievement. Abigail Fisher, a white student who did not qualify for admission under the TTP program, sued, claiming that she would have been admitted had race not been a factor and that the admissions

---

[39] 132 S. Ct. 1536 (2012).

[40] 78 F.3d 932, 944 (5th Cir. 1996).

program was therefore unconstitutional.[41] The Fifth Circuit upheld UT's admissions plan,[42] but Fisher appealed, and the Supreme Court agreed to review the case.[43]

Ultimately, Fisher is arguing that the Court should invalidate UT's admissions plan under one of two different theories: (1) by finding that UT's consideration of race violates the standards set forth in *Grutter*; or (2) by finding that racial diversity in higher education is no longer a compelling governmental interest, thus overruling *Grutter* entirely. Texas has countered that its "individualized and holistic" admissions plan serves a compelling interest in achieving racial diversity and is narrowly tailored to meet that interest.[44] Notably, the Court's composition has changed in the years since the University of Michigan cases were decided, with the departure of Justice O'Connor, who provided the fifth vote to uphold the law school's plan in *Grutter*. Three of the four dissenters in *Grutter* remain on the Court—Justices Kennedy, Scalia, and Thomas— and these three Justices were joined by Justices Roberts and Alito in the 2007 *Parents Involved in Community Schools v. Seattle School District No. 1* decision striking down the racial diversity plans of two elementary and secondary school districts because they did not serve a compelling interest.[45] Given these changes in the Court's composition, UT's admissions program may therefore be in jeopardy. The Court is expected to issue its decision sometime during the 2012-2013 term.

Desegregation and Racial Diversity in Public Elementary, Secondary, and Magnet Schools (K-12)

The use of different cutoff scores for admission of white and minority students to magnet or other special schools within a public school system that formerly was illegally segregated has been the source of considerable controversy. In 1974, for example, courts found the Boston schools to be unlawfully segregated and ordered into effect a desegregation plan requiring, among other things, a 35% set-aside for admission of black and Hispanic students to the city's three "examination" schools.[46] This policy was revised to eliminate the set-aside after a successful equal protection challenge was brought in 1996 by a white student who was denied admission to the famed Boston Latin School.[47] Under the new policy, half of the available seats at each school was awarded solely on the basis of students' composite scores, derived from grade point averages and entrance examination scores. The other half was also awarded according to composite score rankings, but in conjunction with "flexible racial/ethnic guidelines." The guidelines required that these seats be allocated by composite rank score in proportion to the racial and ethnic composition of each school's remaining qualified applicant pool. A white student denied admission for the 1997-1998 academic year, despite higher qualifications than several admitted minority students, challenged the guidelines on equal protection grounds.

---

[41] Brief for Petitioner, Fisher v. Univ. of Texas, 132 S. Ct. 1536 (2012) (No. 11-345).

[42] Fisher v. Univ. of Tex., 631 F.3d 213 (5th Cir. 2011).

[43] 132 S. Ct. 1536 (2012).

[44] Brief for Respondents at 18, Fisher v. Univ. of Texas, 132 S. Ct. 1536 (2012) (No. 11-345).

[45] Parents Involved in Cmty. Sch. v. Seattle Sch. Dist. No. 1, 551 U.S. 701 (2007).

[46] See Morgan v. Hennigan, 379 F. Supp. 410 (D. Mass), aff'd sub nom. Morgan v. Kerrigan, 509 F.2d 580 (lst Cir. 1974).

[47] See McLaughlin v. Boston School Committee, 938 F. Supp. 1001 (D.Mass. 1996).

In *Wessman v. Gittens*,[48] the First Circuit reversed a judgment in favor of the Boston School Committee, which had adopted the two-track admissions policy. The district court had applied strict scrutiny, but nonetheless concluded that the policy was constitutional based on the school system's compelling interests in diversity and in "overcoming the vestiges of past discrimination and avoiding the re-segregation of the Boston Public Schools." According to the appeals court, however, the School Committee had not produced sufficient evidence to demonstrate a compelling interest in either goal or that the admissions policy was narrowly tailored to those ends. First, there was no "solid and compelling evidence" that student diversity was "in any way tied to the vigorous exchange of ideas," nor that any achievement gap between minority and non-minority students amounted to "vestiges" of the system's past discrimination. The policy also swept "too broadly" by dividing individuals into "only five groups—blacks, whites, Hispanic, Asians, and Native Americans—without recognizing that none is monolithic." Thus, even assuming that diversity might, in some circumstances, be sufficiently compelling to justify race-conscious actions, "the School Committee's flexible racial/ethnic guidelines appear to be less a means of attaining diversity in any constitutionally relevant sense and more a means of racial balancing," which is neither "a legitimate [n]or necessary means of advancing the lofty principles credited in the policy."[49]

Meanwhile, in a pair of decisions, the Fourth Circuit invalidated affirmative action policies for admission of minority students to magnet schools in Arlington County, VA, and Montgomery County, MD. Because neither policy was found to satisfy the "narrow tailoring" aspect of strict scrutiny as required by *Adarand*, however, it was unnecessary for the court to decide whether educational diversity may be a "compelling interest" justifying race based admissions in other circumstances. At issue in the Arlington County case, *Tuttle v. Arlington County School Board*,[50] was a "sequential, weighted random lottery" system developed in response to prior litigation which took account of three factors—low-income background, the applicant's primary language, and race or ethnicity—in determining admission to three county magnet schools. The probabilities associated with each applicant's lottery number were weighted, so that members of under-represented groups, as defined by any of those factors, had an increased probability of selection. In the Montgomery County case, *Eisenberg v. Montgomery County Public Schools*,[51] school officials considered a variety of factors, including a "diversity profile" of affected schools, when deciding whether to grant applications for transfer from a student's assigned school to another county public school. The diversity profile, in effect, precluded transfer of students of a particular racial or ethnic background—white, black, Asian, or Hispanic—from any school where the percentage of that group in the student body had declined over the preceding three years and was under-represented when compared to the county as a whole. In both cases, the challenged policy led to white students being denied admission to schools of their choice for racial reasons tied to student diversity.

While the Arlington County school system, earlier in its history, had been found to be *de jure* segregated and was required to desegregate by judicial decree, Montgomery County had never been subject to court-supervised desegregation. Rather, the Maryland district had dismantled its formerly segregated schools by voluntary means, one aspect of which included implementation of a magnet school program. In neither case, however, did the Fourth Circuit attribute a remedial

---

[48] 160 F.3d 790 (1st Cir. 1998).

[49] *Id.* at 799.

[50] 195 F.3d 698 (4th Cir. 1999), cert. denied 529 U.S. 1050 (2000).

[51] 197 F.3d 123 (4th Cir. 1999), cert. denied 529 U.S. 1019 (2000).

purpose to the diversity interest asserted by the school board, but found that the admissions and transfer policies in question were an exercise in "racial balancing." In so doing, the appeals court sidestepped deciding whether racial diversity in education could ever be a "compelling" state interest, proceeding instead to find the challenged policies failed the narrow tailoring aspect of *Adarand* analysis. In the Arlington case, the school board was found to have disregarded "one or more race-neutral policies" recommended by an advisory committee as alternatives to promote diversity. The duration of the plan was criticized for being "in perpetuity" and without "a logical stopping point." Although the weighted lottery did not "set-aside" positions for minorities, according to the court, the practical effect was the same since it "skew[ed] the odds of selection" in their favor to achieve classroom diversity "in proportions that approximate the distribution of students from [racial] groups in the district's overall student population." Finally, the plan lacked flexibility and impermissibly burdened "innocent third parties" who are denied admission for racial or ethnic reasons. Montgomery County's race-conscious transfer policy was characterized by the court as "mere racial balancing in a pure form" due to many of the same failings and because it was not directed at the correction of any past constitutional wrongs.

> The County annually ascertains the percentage of enrolled public school students by race on a county-wide basis, and then does the same for each school. It then assigns a numbered category for each race at each school, and administers the transfer policy so that the race and percentage in each school to which students are assigned by residence is compared to the percentage of that race in the countywide system. The transfer policy is administered with an object toward maintaining this percentage of racial balance in each school.... Although the transfer policy does not necessarily apply 'hard and fast quotas,' its goal of keeping certain percentages of racial/ethnic groups within each school to ensure diversity is racial balancing.[52]

Montgomery County officials were directed to eliminate the consideration of race from student transfer decisions, while in the Arlington case, further proceedings in the district court were ordered to review alternative admissions policies.

The U.S. Supreme Court in 2002 denied review of the Fourth Circuit *en banc* decision in *Belk v. Charlotte Mecklenburg Board of Education*.[53] The appeals court there affirmed a finding that "all vestiges of past discrimination" had been erased from the school system where student busing was first approved by the Supreme Court as a desegregation remedy. Because of its newly achieved "unitary status," the district court had relinquished jurisdiction of the desegregation case and ordered the school district to stop "assigning children to schools or allocating educational opportunities and benefits through race-based lotteries, preferences, set-asides or other means that deny students an equal footing based on race." The specific target of the judge's order was the "race-conscious policy for admission of students to the magnet school program operated by the district for desegregation purposes."[54]

---

[52] *Id.* at 133.

[53] 269 F.3d 305 (4th Cir. 2001), cert. denied, 535 U.S. 986 (2002).

[54] After nearly three decades of court-enforced desegregation, a white parent sued the school district, charging that his daughter had twice been denied admittance to a magnet school because she was not black. Six other white parents joined the case, arguing that the school district had been successfully rid of segregation and with it any constitutional justification for race-based preferences. The judge agreed, calling the argument for continuing the desegregation process a "bizarre posture" and the focus on racial diversity a "social experiment." The policy of allocating available magnet school spaces to reflect the racial student makeup of the district as a whole was condemned by the court as "nothing more than a means for racial balancing," which could not be justified by a "litany of generalizations lauding the benefits of racial diversity."

A majority of the *en banc* appellate court affirmed that the school district had eliminated the "last vestiges" of unconstitutional segregation to the fullest extent "practicable." Any remaining racial concentrations, therefore; were a consequence of factors—namely residential segregation— beyond the power of school authorities or the courts to control. In a unitary setting, the magnet admissions process could not clear the first hurdle by showing a compelling governmental interest, and the school district could not make "any further use of race-based lotteries, preferences, and set-asides in student assignment." A slightly different majority ruled that the school board could not be held liable for its use of race in assigning students to magnet schools since the program had originated in a then valid desegregation order. But if the same plan were adopted after the district is declared unitary, it would clearly be unconstitutional under *Tuttle* and *Eisenberg*, these judges opined.

The issue before the Fourth Circuit in *Belk* focused on whether the school board, in creating its admission plan, was acting beyond what was permitted to comply with the court's desegregation order. Another ruling, by the Fifth Circuit, in *Cavalier v. Caddo Parish School Board*,[55] also suggests that educational authorities have broader discretion to consider race in making admissions decisions when the school district is under a court order to desegregate. *Cavalier* held that a magnet school preferential admissions program that mandated a 50% to 50% (plus or minus 15%) racial student mix, and imposed lower minimum standardized test scores for minority than white applicants, was not narrowly tailored to a compelling governmental interest. The school board relied exclusively on a 1981 consent decree ordering desegregation to prove a compelling governmental interest. Magnet schools had been released from the decree in 1990, however. And the appeals court found that while student body diversity provided compelling justification for considering race in law school admissions under *Grutter*, "it is by no means clear that it could be such at or below the high school level."[56] The admission plan was additionally flawed for its failure to consider race-neutral means to achieve student body diversity and was a quota system. Student selections were made from two separate lists of applicant students, one for black students and one for white students, without direct comparison of candidates to the applicant pool at large. Insulating students of one racial group from competition with the larger admissions pool, along with the 50% goal, amounted to an impermissible quota.

The diversity issue has also arisen in another educational setting. The University of California operates a popular elementary school as a "laboratory" to research urban education and "to foster a more effective educational system primarily for urban elementary students." Beyond basic research, the school develops new techniques for educating students in multi-cultural urban settings and conducts seminars, workshops, and teacher training programs throughout the state. The school considers applicants' race and ethnicity to obtain adequate cross-samples of the general population and thus to maintain "the scientific credibility of its educational studies." The plaintiff in *Hunter v. Regents of the University of California*[57] challenged the school's admissions policy as an equal protection violation. While perhaps not tantamount to a diversity rationale, the Ninth Circuit nonetheless agreed with the district court judge that the state's interest in "operating a research-oriented elementary school dedicated to improving the quality of education in urban public schools" was compelling even absent any purpose of remedying past discrimination.

---

[55] 403 F.3d 246 (5th Cir. 2005).

[56] *Id.* at 259.

[57] 190 F.3d 1061 (9th Cir. 1999), cert. denied, 531 U.S. 877 (2000).

> The challenges posed by California's increasingly diverse population intensify the state's interest in improving urban public schools. Cultural and economic differences in the classroom pose special difficulties for public school teachers. In his decision, Judge Kenyon noted that defendants presented "an exhaustive list of such issues and challenges [that] includes limited language proficiency, different learning styles, involvement of parents from diverse cultures with different expectations and values, and racial and ethnic conflict among families and children." [An expert witness] stated that "[t]here is no more pressing problem, facing California, or indeed the nation, than urban education; for it is in the urban school system that the majority of California's future citizens will be educated (either well or poorly), creating the basic fabric for the society of the future." ... Given this record, the district court concluded, and we agree, that "the defendants' interest in operating a research-oriented elementary school is compelling."[58]

Given the demographics of California's urban population, and the necessity of creating a multi-cultural laboratory setting, the consideration of race for admission to the school was deemed "narrowly tailored" since "it would not be possible, nor would it be reasonable, to require defendants to attempt to obtain an ethnically diverse representative sample of students without specific racial target and classifications."[59]

Meanwhile, although the Supreme Court in *Grutter* did not address the voluntary use of race as a factor in achieving diversity in elementary and secondary education, all three appeals courts to consider the issue after *Grutter* and *Gratz* were decided upheld racial diversity measures in public schools.[60] In *Comfort v. Lynn School Committee*,[61] the First Circuit issued an *en banc* decision holding that a school district use of race as a factor in its student assignment plan does not violate the Equal Protection Clause. Relying on principles laid down by *Grutter* and *Gratz*, the First Circuit concluded that the plan's goal of securing the educational benefits of racial diversity constituted a compelling interest and that the plan was narrowly tailored to achieve that goal. The ruling reversed an earlier three-judge appellate panel's contrary conclusion that the consideration of race in Lynn's voluntary school choice plan was unconstitutional.

Under Massachusetts's Racial Imbalance Act, local communities received additional state education aid if they adopted plans that assigned students on the basis of race. The City of Lynn School Committee implemented a voluntary desegregation plan that allowed all students to attend neighborhood schools. Race only became a factor when a student sought to transfer to another school. The transfer was permitted only if it would not increase the racial imbalance at either the sending or receiving school. Citizens for the Preservation of Constitutional Rights (CPCR) filed suit on behalf of several parents. A federal district court ruled that the plan satisfied equal protection requirements. On appeal, the three-judge panel reversed the district court, ruling that while the goal of student body diversity constituted a compelling state interest, the plan was not narrowly tailored to that end.

The panel decision was withdrawn when the First Circuit granted Lynn's motion for a rehearing *en banc*. Addressing the "compelling state interest" prong of the equal protection test, the full

---

[58] *Id.* at 1064.

[59] *Id.* at 1065.

[60] The holdings in these cases have presumably been invalidated by the Court's subsequent ruling in *Parents Involved in Community Schools*.

[61] 418 F.3d 1 (1st Cir. 2005).

court measured the plan against the law school admissions policy upheld in *Grutter*. The court rejected CPCR's assertion that *Grutter's* recognition of a compelling interest in

> "the educational benefits that flow from student body diversity" ... is ... limited to the benefits that flow from viewpoint diversity in the higher education context and does not extend to the benefits that flow from racial diversity in the K-12 context.

The First Circuit, however, found that the educational benefits found compelling in *Grutter* were advanced not only by viewpoint diversity, but also by racial diversity, and these interests were no less strong in K-12 than in higher education.

Turning to the "narrowly tailored " prong, the court noted that while the Supreme Court had yet to consider the question, *Grutter* and *Gratz* provided sufficient guidance to determine the constitutionality of a voluntary K-12 race-based assignment policy. Because the Lynn plan dealt with a noncompetitive transfer policy, as opposed to competitive admissions policies, competition-related criteria—such as need for individualized consideration of applicants, so important in *Grutter/Gratz*—were not relevant here. Otherwise, the court found that the plan's use of race was minimally invasive; avoided racial balancing for its own sake; avoided use of quotas; was of finite duration; and was adopted after considering race-neutral alternatives.

In *MacFarland v. Jefferson County Public Schools*,[62] issued on the first anniversary of the Michigan decisions and the 50th anniversary of *Brown v. Board of Education*, a federal district court in Kentucky upheld a Louisville district's voluntary consideration of race in making student assignments to achieve racial integration in the public schools. Jefferson County Public Schools (JCPS) were ordered by judicial decree to desegregate in 1975. Under the desegregation plan, each school was to have between 15% and 50% African-American enrollment and students were bused, if necessary, to ensure racial diversity. Twenty-five years later, in 2000, the federal courts ended their supervision of the desegregation plan, but the JCPS voluntarily opted to maintain its integrated schools through a "managed choice" plan. The plan was challenged in a lawsuit by black parents whose children were denied admission to Central High School, which was already at the upper percentage limit for minority enrollment.

The district court found that the managed choice plan served numerous compelling state interests, "some of the same reasons for integrated schools that the Supreme Court upheld in *Grutter*." Thus, Judge Heyburn accepted the school board's arguments that the plan improved the educational experience; that it produced educational benefits for students of all races over the last 25 years; and that it helped overcome the adverse effects of concentrations of poverty that impact black students to a greater extent than whites. "Integrated schools, better academic performance, appreciation for our diverse heritage and stronger, more competitive public schools are consistent with the central values and themes of American culture," Judge Heyburn wrote. The court also found that the student assignment plan was "narrowly tailored" in every respect except for its use of separate "racial categories," which the district was required to revise for the 2005-2006 school year. For reasons "articulated in the well-reasoned opinion of the district court," the Sixth Circuit summarily affirmed Judge Heyburn's decree, without issuing a detailed written opinion.[63]

---

[62] 330 F. Supp. 2d 834 (W.D.Ky. 2004).

[63] McFarland v. Jefferson County Public Schools, 416 F.3d 513 (6th Cir. 2003).

The constitutionality of race-conscious admissions to magnet or alternative schools, designed to promote elementary and secondary school desegregation, has also been before the courts. In *Parents Involved in Community Schools v. Seattle School District No. 1*,[64] the Ninth Circuit applied *Grutter* and *Gratz* to approve a school district's plan to maintain racially diverse schools. Under Seattle's "controlled choice" high school student assignment plan, students were given the option to attend high schools across the district, but if the demand for seats exceeded the supply at a particular school, a student's race was considered as a tie-breaker in determining admittance to the oversubscribed school. The racial tie-breaker applied only to schools whose student bodies deviated by more than 15 percentage points from the overall racial makeup of the district, then "approximately 40% white and 60% nonwhite." The Seattle plan was voluntarily adopted to "achiev[e] diversity [and] limit racial isolation" in the schools, not as a part of a desegregation remedy.

In an *en banc* decision, the Ninth Circuit ruled that the school district had a compelling interest in the educational and social benefits of racial diversity and in avoiding racially concentrated or isolated schools. Further, the court held that the district's plan was sufficiently narrowly tailored to pass constitutional muster. According to the court, the "individualized" and "holistic" review endorsed by the Supreme Court was not required of a noncompetitive, voluntary student assignment plan such as Seattle's, as long as the plan was otherwise narrowly tailored. The court held that Seattle's plan was sufficiently narrowly tailored, concluding that the 15 percentage point "band" was not a quota because it was flexible and did not reserve a certain number of fixed slots based on race. The court also ruled that the school district had made a good faith effort to consider race-neutral alternatives. Finally, the court concluded that the plan imposed a minimal burden—not being permitted to attend one's preferred school—that was shared by all students and that the plan, which was subject to regular reviews, was sufficiently limited in time and in scope. The ruling reversed an earlier three-judge appellate panel's contrary decision that the school district's plan to maintain racially diverse schools was not sufficiently narrowly tailored.

As noted above, the Supreme Court had never, until recently, considered the constitutionality of the voluntary use of race as a factor in achieving diversity in elementary and secondary education. All three of the federal appeals courts to consider the issue since *Grutter* and *Gratz* were decided upheld racial diversity measures in public schools,[65] but these opinions conflicted with pre-*Grutter/Gratz* appellate rulings that rejected such racially based plans.[66] Possibly as a result of this conflict, the Supreme Court granted review in *MacFarland v. Jefferson County Public Schools*—now *Meredith v. Jefferson County Board of Education*—and *Parents Involved in Community Schools v. Seattle School District No. 1* to consider the question of what steps, if any, a public school district may take to maintain racial diversity in elementary and secondary education.[67] In *Parents Involved in Community Schools v. Seattle School District No. 1*, a consolidated ruling that resolved both cases, the Court ultimately struck down the school plans at issue, holding that they violated the equal protection guarantee of the Fourteenth Amendment.[68]

---

[64] 426 F. 3d 1162 (9th Cir. 2005).

[65] Comfort v. Lynn Sch. Comm., 418 F.3d 1 (1st Cir. 2005); McFarland v. Jefferson County Pub. Schs., 416 F.3d 513 (6th Cir. 2005); Parents Involved in Cmty. Sch. v. Seattle Sch. Dist., No. 1, 426 F.3d 1162 (9th Cir. 2005).

[66] See, e.g., Tuttle v. Arlington County Sch. Bd., 195 F.3d 698 (4th Cir. 1999); Eisenberg ex rel. Eisenberg v. Montgomery County Pub. Schs., 197 F.3d 123 (4th Cir. 1999); Wessmann v. Gittens, 160 F.3d 790 (1st Cir. 1998).

[67] 547 U.S. 1177 (2006).

[68] 551 U.S. 701 (2007).

The *Parents Involved in Community Schools* Decision

Ultimately, the Supreme Court held that the Louisville and Seattle school plans violated the equal protection clause. However, the decision was fractured, with five different Justices filing opinions in the case. Announcing the judgment of the Court was Chief Justice Roberts, who led a plurality of four Justices in concluding that the school plans were unconstitutional because they did not serve a compelling governmental interest. Although Justice Kennedy, who concurred in the Court's judgment striking down the plans, disagreed with the plurality's conclusion that the diversity plans did not serve a compelling governmental interest, he found that the school plans were unconstitutional because they were not narrowly tailored. In addition, Justice Thomas filed a concurring opinion, and Justices Stevens and Breyer filed separate dissenting opinions.

In the portion of his opinion that was joined by Justice Kennedy and that therefore announced the judgment of the Court, Chief Justice Roberts began by noting that the Court had jurisdiction in the case, thereby rejecting a challenge to the standing of the plaintiff organization Parents Involved in Community Schools (PICS).[69] Chief Justice Roberts then turned to the substantive merits of the claims involved, reiterating that governmental racial classifications must be reviewed under strict scrutiny. As a result, the Court examined whether the school districts had demonstrated that their assignment and transfer plans were narrowly tailored to achieve a compelling governmental interest.

In assessing the compelling interest prong of the strict scrutiny test, Chief Justice Roberts noted that the Court has recognized two interests that qualify as compelling where the use of racial classifications in the school context is concerned: remedying the effects of past intentional discrimination and promoting diversity in higher education. However, the Chief Justice found that neither of these interests was advanced by the school plans at issue. According to the Chief Justice, because Seattle schools were never intentionally segregated and because the lifting of its desegregation order demonstrated that Louisville schools had successfully remediated past discrimination in its schools, neither school district could assert a compelling interest in remedying past intentional discrimination.[70]

Likewise, the Court argued that the *Grutter* precedent did not govern the current cases. According to Chief Justice Roberts, the compelling interest recognized in *Grutter* was in a broadly defined diversity that encompassed more than just racial diversity and that focused on each applicant as an individual. Because race was the only factor considered by the school districts rather than other factors that reflected a broader spectrum of diverse qualifications and characteristics and because the plans did not provide individualized review of applicants, the plurality opinion found that the school districts' articulated interest in diversity was not compelling. Added the Chief Justice, "[e]ven when it comes to race, the plans here employ only a limited notion of diversity, viewing race exclusively in white/nonwhite terms in Seattle and black/'other' terms in Jefferson County."[71] In rejecting *Grutter* as applicable precedent, the Court also noted that the decision had rested in part on the unique considerations of higher education and that those considerations were absent in the elementary and secondary education context.

---

[69] Parents Involved in Cmty. Sch. v. Seattle Sch. Dist. No. 1, 551 U.S. 701, 718-20 (2007).

[70] *Id.* at 721-22.

[71] *Id.* at 723.

Even if the school districts had met the first prong of the strict scrutiny test by establishing a compelling governmental interest in the use of racial classifications to make school assignments, the Court found the school plans would still have failed the second prong of the test because they were not sufficiently narrowly tailored to meet their stated goals. According to Chief Justice Roberts, in both Seattle and Louisville, only a few students were assigned to a non-preferred school based on race. As a result, "the minimal impact of the districts' racial classifications on school enrollment casts doubt on the necessity of using racial classifications,"[72] especially in light of the fact that such racial classifications are permissible in only the most extreme circumstances. Additionally, the Court was concerned that the school districts had failed to consider methods other than racial classifications to achieve their goals, despite a requirement that narrowly tailored programs consider race-neutral alternatives.

Although Justice Kennedy joined the above portions of the plurality opinion, thereby forming a majority in favor of striking down the school plans, he did not join the remainder of the plurality opinion, which concluded for additional reasons that the school plans were unconstitutional. In these portions of his opinion, Chief Justice Roberts faulted the school plans for tying their diversity goals to each district's specific racial demographics rather than to "any pedagogical concept of the level of diversity needed to obtain the asserted educational benefits."[73] In other words, each district tried to establish schools with racial diversity that mirrored the percentages of racial groups in their respective overall populations. This effort, according to the Chief Justice, amounted to unconstitutional racial balancing because the plans were not in fact narrowly tailored to the goal of achieving the educational and social benefits that allegedly flow from racial diversity but rather were tailored to racial demographics instead. Indeed, Chief Justice Roberts wrote, "[a]ccepting racial balancing as a compelling state interest would justify the imposition of racial proportionality throughout American society, contrary to our repeated recognition that at the heart of the Constitution's guarantee of equal protection lies the simple command that the Government must treat citizens as individuals, not as simply components of a racial, religious, sexual or national class."[74] Such racial balancing could not, in the Chief Justice's view, amount to a compelling governmental interest even if pursued in the name of racial diversity or racial integration.

In another portion of the plurality opinion not joined by Justice Kennedy, Chief Justice Roberts criticized Justice Breyer's dissent for misapplying precedents that recognized a compelling interest in remedying past discrimination. According to the Chief Justice, the Court has recognized a compelling interest in remedying past discrimination when that discrimination is caused by governmental action but not when caused by other factors, such as social or economic pressures. Noting that the Seattle school district was never segregated due to state action and the Louisville school district had eliminated all vestiges of state segregation, the Chief Justice therefore argued that the cases cited by Justice Breyer as precedents for race-conscious school integration efforts were inapplicable to the current case.[75] The plurality opinion concluded with a discussion of *Brown v. Board of Education*,[76] in which the Court held that the deliberate segregation of schoolchildren by race was unconstitutional. According to the plurality:

---

[72] *Id.* at 734.

[73] *Id.* at 726.

[74] *Id.* at 730.

[75] *Id.* at 735-40.

[76] 347 U.S. 483 (1954).

> Before *Brown*, schoolchildren were told where they could and could not go to school based
> on the color of their skin. The school districts in these cases have not carried the heavy
> burden of demonstrating that we should allow this once again—even for very different
> reasons.... The way to stop discrimination on the basis of race is to stop discriminating on the
> basis of race.[77]

Although he joined the Court in striking down the school plans, Justice Kennedy wrote a separate
concurring opinion that provides additional insight into how the Justices might handle future
cases involving the consideration of race in the educational context. As noted above, Justice
Kennedy declined to sign on to the plurality opinion in full, in part because he disagreed with its
implication that diversity in elementary and secondary education, at least as properly defined,
does not serve a compelling governmental interest. According to Justice Kennedy, "[d]iversity,
depending on its meaning and definition, is a compelling educational goal a school district may
pursue,"[78] but neither Seattle nor Louisville had shown that its plans served a compelling interest
in promoting diversity or that the plans were narrowly tailored to achieve that goal.

Justice Kennedy also pointedly criticized the plurality opinion for "imply[ing] an all-too-
unyielding insistence that race cannot be a factor in instances when, in my view, it may be taken
into account.... In the administration of public schools by the state and local authorities, it is
permissible to consider the racial makeup of schools and to adopt general policies to encourage a
diverse student body, one aspect of which is its racial composition."[79] Justice Kennedy identified
several ways in which schools, in his view, could constitutionally pursue racial diversity or avoid
racial isolation, including strategic site selection of new schools, altering attendance zones,
providing resources for special programs, and recruiting students and faculty. According to
Justice Kennedy, such measures would be constitutional because, while race-conscious, they are
not based on classifications that treat individuals differently based on race. However, Justice
Kennedy would not limit schools to facially neutral methods of achieving diversity, saying that
racial classifications might be permissible if based on "a more nuanced, individual evaluation of
school needs and student characteristics" similar to the plan approved in *Grutter*.[80] Although no
other Justice joined his concurrence, Justice Kennedy's unique role in providing the pivotal swing
vote in the case makes his concurring opinion significant to any future legal developments
regarding the use of racial classifications in the education context.

Although Justice Thomas joined the plurality opinion written by Chief Justice Roberts in full, he
also wrote a separate concurring opinion that took issue with certain aspects of Justice Breyer's
dissent. Among other things, Justice Thomas disagreed with the dissent's assertion that the school
plans were necessary to combat school resegregation, arguing that neither Seattle nor Louisville
faced the type of intentional state action to separate the races that the school districts in *Brown*
had.[81] In addition, Justice Thomas contested the dissent's argument that a less strict standard of
review should apply when racial classifications are used for benign purposes, in part because
Justice Thomas disagreed that the school plans—which, he wrote, inevitably exclude some
individuals based on race and therefore may exacerbate racial tension—are as benign as the
dissent asserted. More importantly, Justice Thomas argued that the perception of what constitutes

---

[77] Parents Involved in Cmty. Schs. v. Seattle Sch. Dist. No. 1, 551 U.S. at 747-48.

[78] *Id.* at 783.

[79] *Id.* at 787-88.

[80] *Id.* at 790.

[81] *Id.* at 749-50.

a benign use of race-conscious measures is nothing more than a reflection of current social practice that relies too heavily on the good intentions of current public officials. According to Justice Thomas, "if our history has taught us anything, it has taught us to beware of elites bearing racial theories," adding in a footnote, "Justice Breyer's good intentions, which I do not doubt, have the shelf life of Justice Breyer's tenure."[82]

As noted above, both Justices Stevens and Breyer dissented from the Court's decision to strike down the school plans. In his brief dissent, Justice Stevens, who also joined Justice Breyer's dissent, described the Court's reliance on *Brown* as a "cruel irony" because it ignored the historical context in which *Brown* was decided and the ways in which subsequent precedents applied the landmark decision to uphold school integration efforts.[83] Meanwhile, in a lengthy and passionate dissent nearly twice as long as Chief Justice Roberts's opinion, Justice Breyer argued that the Court's holding

> distorts precedent, ... misapplies the relevant constitutional principles, ... announces legal rules that will obstruct efforts by state and local governments to deal effectively with the growing resegregation of public schools, ... threatens to substitute for present calm a disruptive round of race-related litigation, and ... undermines *Brown's* promise of integrated primary and secondary education that local communities have sought to make a reality.[84]

Faculty Diversity

Corollary issues concerning faculty diversity have also been before the courts, including the *Piscataway* case, which was dismissed as moot by the Supreme Court after the parties reached an out-of-court settlement. The appeal from *Taxman v. Board of Education of Piscataway Township*[85] had asked the High Court to consider whether a local school board's desire to promote faculty diversity could legally justify its decision to protect a black teacher from layoff, while dismissing an equally qualified white colleague, in the absence of a showing of past discrimination or a "manifest" racial imbalance in its workforce. Two teachers, one white, the other black, were hired on the same day in 1980 and were deemed equally qualified for their positions in the business education department when a reduction in force became necessary eight years later. Minority teachers were not underrepresented on the overall faculty—constituting 9.5% of the district's teachers versus 5.8% of the relevant county labor pool—and no evidence of past discrimination by the school district was presented at trial. A "coin toss" had traditionally been used to determine retention rights among similarly situated employees in the past. But because only one black teacher was among the business department's 10-member staff, the school district relied on its affirmative action policy to retain the minority employee rather than her white colleague in the interests of promoting racial diversity.

An *en banc* majority of the Third Circuit determined that however laudable the school board's objective might be, laying off a white teacher "solely" on the basis of race to achieve faculty diversity exceeded the bounds of controlling Supreme Court precedent. Title VII rulings in *Weber* and *Johnson* permitted employers to make employment decisions based on race or gender in

---

[82] *Id.* at 782, n. 30.

[83] *Id.* at 798-803.

[84] *Id.* at 803-04.

[85] 91 F.3d 1547 (3d Cir. 1996), appeal dismissed sub nom. Piscataway Twp. Bd. of Educ. v. Taxman, 522 U.S. 1010 (1997).

order to redress a "manifest" imbalance of minorities and women in "traditionally segregated job categories." But judicial teachings generally caution against affirmative action measures that "unnecessarily trammel" or frustrate the "legitimate and firmly rooted expectation in continued employment" of affected non-minorities. In its 1986 *Wygant* decision, the Court voided race-based layoff protection for minority public school teachers because of its immediate adverse impact on "identifiable" senior white employees. Consequently, while applauding the board's commitment to racial diversity, the *Taxman* appellate opinion rejected the non-remedial educational purposes asserted by the board for its affirmative action plan because "there is no congressional recognition of diversity as a Title VII objective requiring accommodation." And because the entire burden of the board's plan fell upon the white teacher whose interests were "unnecessarily trammeled" by the loss of her job, the race-based policy violated Title VII.

In 1998, the Supreme Court declined to review the legality of a "minority bonus policy" in an affirmative action plan established for Nevada's public colleges to redress a lack of minority faculty members. In *Farmer v. University and Community College Systems of Nevada*,[86] the plaintiff had been one of three finalists for a faculty position in the sociology department that the university awarded to a black male candidate from Uganda with "comparable" qualifications. The university's minority bonus policy, which the Nevada Supreme Court described as an "unwritten amendment" to its affirmative action plan, allowed a department to hire an additional faculty member following the initial placement of a minority candidate. As a consequence, the plaintiff was hired by the sociology department a year later, but at a lesser salary than the earlier-hired black candidate. The differential was defended by the university as reflecting a pay premium necessary "to prevent[ ] a bidding war between two prestigious universities slated to interview [the black candidate]." Farmer challenged both the hiring and pay decisions by the university as race and sex discrimination prohibited by Title VII and the Equal Pay Act.

The state supreme court reversed a jury verdict for the plaintiff and upheld the university's affirmative action hiring policy on both federal constitutional and statutory grounds. First, according to the court, race was only one factor considered by the university—along with educational background, publishing, teaching experience, etc.—in evaluating applicants. In contrast to *Piscataway*, the university faculty was a "white enclave" with only 1% black members, a factor persuading the court that the university had a "compelling interest in fostering a culturally and ethnically diverse faculty" under standards laid out by the *Bakke* and *Weber* cases.

> Here, in addition to considerations of race, the University based its employment decision on such criteria as educational background, publishing, teaching experience, and areas of specialization. This satisfies *Bakke*'s commands that race must be only one of several factors used in evaluating applicants. We also view the desirability of a racially diverse faculty as sufficiently analogous to the constitutionally permissible attainment of a racially diverse student body countenanced by the *Bakke* Court.

Thus, severe minority underrepresentation on the university faculty combined with the employer's consideration of relative qualifications in addition to race distinguished *Piscataway*, the Nevada court felt, and conformed the case to Justice Powell's *Bakke* opinion. In addition, the impact of the initial minority hire was mitigated by affording the disappointed white applicant a subsequent position created pursuant to informal practice or custom under the affirmative action policy.

---

[86] 930 P.2d 730 (Nev. 1997), cert. denied 523 U.S. 1004 (1998).

IV. Conclusion

The Michigan cases resolved an issue that had vexed the lower federal courts for a quarter-century. Historically, judicial insistence on strict scrutiny has largely condemned governmental distinctions based on race, except in the most narrowly circumscribed circumstances. To the short list of governmental interests sufficiently "compelling" to warrant race-based decision-making, a majority of the Court added the pursuit of diversity in higher education. But this expansion has been curtailed somewhat by the Court's more recent pronouncement involving elementary and secondary school plans to promote racial diversity and its decision to revisit affirmative action in higher education in the upcoming *Fisher* case.

Although the Court's decision to strike down the Seattle and Louisville school assignment and transfer plans will have a profound impact on similar plans at many of the nation's elementary and secondary schools, the *Parents Involved in Community Schools* case did not completely foreclose the possibility that school districts may constitutionally pursue certain measures to avoid racial isolation, prevent resegregation, and promote racial diversity in their schools. However, it is not entirely clear what these measures might entail. While the facially race-neutral methods identified in Justice Kennedy's concurring opinion—such as engaging in strategic site selection of new schools, altering attendance zones, providing resources for special programs, and recruiting students and faculty—seem more likely to survive judicial scrutiny, the fate of other kinds of race-conscious school plans may become apparent only as a result of legal developments that emerge over time. Indeed, there is evidence that some school districts are abandoning race-based school assignment plans in favor of plans based on socioeconomic status, which is a non-suspect classification for purposes of constitutional review.[87] Likewise, some colleges and universities have taken similar steps in anticipation of judicial rulings limiting the use of race in higher education.[88]

Meanwhile, the seeds of future controversy may lie in questions arguably raised but not fully addressed by the latest rulings. For example, the Court's latest rulings left unanswered the constitutional status of racially exclusive diversity policies not directly involving admissions, such as the legality of race-based scholarship and financial aid, recruitment and outreach, or college preparation courses that exclusively target minority populations. In addition, the question of whether schools or universities may completely avoid constitutional shoals by adopting "race-neutral" plans to increase racial diversity may not be fully answered by the Court's latest rulings. Such race-neutral alternatives include "percentage plans" like those approved in Texas, Florida, and California that guarantee college admission to top graduates from every state high school, regardless of race. In addition to percentage plans, educational authorities have experimented with other forms of "alternative action," or policies designed to promote racial diversity without relying on racial preferences. "Class-based" affirmative action, for example, takes socioeconomic status or the family educational background of students into account. Florida has replaced race and ethnicity with other socioeconomic and geographical proxies for diversity; increased the state's need-based financial aid program; sought to improve the state's lowest-performing primary and secondary schools; and provided free SAT prep courses at those schools. California state schools have targeted financial aid programs toward underprivileged neighborhoods as a means

---

[87] Emily Bazelon, *The Next Kind of Integration*, N.Y. Times, July 20, 2008, at MM38.

[88] Rosa Ramirez, "Colleges' Plan B for Diversity," *National Journal*, October 11, 2012, at http://www.nationaljournal.com/thenextamerica/education/colleges-plan-b-for-diversity-20121009.

of reaching minority students. Another approach considers "diversity" or "hardship" essays in which applicants describe challenging life experiences such as poverty, English as a second language, or having a family member in prison. Some reformers advocate targeting additional resources to underperforming elementary and secondary schools as a way to address the root causes of minority underrepresentation in higher education.

By avoiding the use of explicit racial classifications and dual track admission policies, these efforts are far less susceptible to facial challenge as an equal protection violation. Programs involving the explicit consideration of race remain most at risk. But policies that employ nonracial factors as a proxy for race may be vulnerable if the purpose or intent is to benefit minority groups. In *Washington v. Davis*[89] and related rulings,[90] the Supreme Court determined that a race-neutral law with a disparate racial impact on minority groups is subject to strict scrutiny if it is enacted with a racially discriminatory purpose. Racial motive was made a constitutional "touchstone" for equal protection analysis, and whether reflected by a racial classification or other evidence of discriminatory purpose, strict scrutiny was triggered by evidence of such intent. Similarly, alternatives to traditional racial diversity policies may not escape strict judicial scrutiny if an objecting non-minority applicant is able to show that the plan was racially motivated. The same limitations may apply to private institutions, which are immune from constitutional limitations, under Title VI of the 1964 Civil Rights Act.

Beyond education, issues may inevitably arise concerning the implications of *Grutter*, *Parents Involved in Community Schools*, and *Fisher* on efforts to achieve racial diversity in other social and economic spheres. To date, the Court has permitted race-conscious hiring criteria by private employers under Title VII, either as a remedy for past discrimination or to redress a "conspicuous racial imbalance in traditionally segregated job categories,"[91] but refused to find that a state's interest in faculty diversity to provide teacher "role models" was sufficiently compelling to warrant a race-conscious layoff policy.[92] Lower courts are similarly divided, though a few have applied an "operational need analysis" to uphold police force diversity policies, recognizing "that 'a law enforcement body's need to carry out its mission effectively, with a workforce that appears unbiased, is able to communicate with the public and is respected by the community it serves,' may constitute a compelling state interest."[93] But current standards under the federal civil rights

---

[89] 426 U.S. 229 (1976).

[90] Cf. Personnel Administrator v. Feeney, 442 U.S. 256 (1979). In Feeney, the Court upheld a state law giving a preference to veterans for civil service employment, which had a significant discriminatory effect against female applicants. Notwithstanding the obvious impact of such a preference, the Court upheld it on the ground that "'[d]iscriminatory purpose' ... implies more than intent as volition or intent as awareness of consequences. It implies that the decisionmaker ... selected or reaffirmed a particular course of action at least in part 'because of,' not merely 'in spite of,' its adverse effects upon an identifiable group." *Id.* at 279. Although Feeney involved a claim of sex-based discrimination, the test there announced for determining whether a purpose is "discriminatory" with respect to a particular trait has been applied to claims of racial discrimination as well. See Hernandez v. New York, 500 U.S. 352, 360 (1991).

[91] United Steelworkers of America v. Weber, 443 U.S. 179 (1979). In Johnson v. Transportation Agency, 480 U.S. 616 (1980), the Court extended this analysis to gender-conscious affirmative action programs in regard to use of a "plus" factor in hiring and promotion decisions.

[92] Wygant v. Board of Education, 476 U.S. 267 (1986).

[93] Patrolmen's Benevolent Assoc. v. City of New York, 310 F.3d 43, 52 (quoting Barhold v. Rodriguez, 863 F.2d 233, 238 (2d Cir. 1988); Reynolds v. City of Chicago, 296 F.3d 524 (7th Cir. 2002). See also Cotter v. City of Boston, 323 F.3d 160, 172 n. 10 (1st Cir. 2003) (declining to address question of compelling interest but expressing sympathy for "the argument that communities place more trust in a diverse police force and that the resulting trust reduces crime rates and improves policing").

laws generally allow for consideration of race in hiring and promotion decisions only in response to demonstrable evidence of past discrimination by the employer or within the affected industry. No rule of deference like that extended to educational institutions has been recognized for employers, nor is one likely to be applied in the wake of *Parents Involved in Community Schools* or *Fisher*.

Author Contact Information

Jody Feder
Legislative Attorney
jfeder@crs.loc.gov, 7-8088

Acknowledgments

This report was originally written by Charles V. Dale, Legislative Attorney.

www.ingramcontent.com/pod-product-compliance
Lightning Source LLC
Chambersburg PA
CBHW081244170526
45165CB00009B/3189